BUILD

UNIVERS

Gideon Samson
Michael Strachan

Identify the flesh from the Holy Spirit

europe books

© 2024 **Europe Books**| London

www.europebooks.co.uk | info@europebooks.co.uk

ISBN 9791220151054

First edition: July 2024

Identify the flesh from the Holy Spirit

INTRODUCTION

T his book does not go against or condemn any religion, Christianity or any other religions that are playing a role in saving humanity from getting totally lost from where we should be, because without not knowing morals from birth we wouldn't be aware that we have done something wrong. This book is also not part of any religion because what we share is our real-life experience. We share love and family to you and for those that need it.

The purpose of life on Earth is not to be comfortable, but to be watchful at choices that create a good or bad reality whilst being here on Earth.

This book was created to share important messages for humanity. It is to help this generation and beyond to become spiritually awakened whilst discussing the spiritual effects of sex, identifying the inner self, outer self, and supernatural self. It teaches about faith and its magical power and how we share it in Christ's glorious body.

The only reason why we have access to time (life) is so that we can build a solid foundation with God before the afterlife, practice goodness with all you're might and hold firm to the word of God. The glory that awaits us is nothing compared to what our human thought can imagine, that is why the scripture says - Christ Crucified:

And I, brethren, when I came to you, did not come with excellence of speech or of wisdom declaring to you the testimony of God. For I determined not to know anything among you except Jesus Christ and him crucified.

I was with you in weakness, in fear, and in much trembling.

And my speech and my preaching were not with persuasive words of human wisdom, but in demonstration of the Spirit and of power, that your faith should not be in the wisdom of men but in the power of God.

"Spiritual Wisdom"

However, we speak wisdom among those who are mature, yet not the wisdom of this age, nor of the rulers of this age, who are coming to nothing. We speak the wisdom of God in a mystery, the hidden wisdom which God ordained before the ages of our glory, which none of the rulers of this age knew; for had they known, they would not have crucified the Lord of glory. But as it is written:

"Eye has not seen, nor ear heard, nor have entered into the heart of the things which God has prepared for those who love him."

But God has revealed them to us through his Spirit. For the Spirit searches all things, yes, the deep things of God. For what man knows the things of a man except the spirit of the man which is in him? Even so no one knows the things of God except the Spirit of God.

Now we have received, not the spirit of the world, but the Spirit who is from God, that we might know the things that have been freely given to us by God.

Amen

GIDEON SAMSON

Before the arrival of Jesus Christ, the spirit of God only visited men who were dedicated and chosen. Most men by faith received answers from God through Angels. A man could not view other than what they could see physically (only a prophet or someone gifted could see past the present). They could not predict the result of their actions because they are moved by their emotions. Every day on Earth our actions during the daytime make us spiritually grow towards the night. When we meditate during the night it is the best time to reflect on yourself. The best way to do this is by giving thanks to God through your thoughts, actions, and speech, it does not mean your thoughts will always feel good but always give the good thoughts and the bad thoughts to God and he will transform them both. God is transparency and if you reflect your heart with proper understanding that he his God, and you are the weak vessel, the right way to speak to him will come.

The scripture says that out of the abundance of the heart the mouth speaks. At mid-morning there is always a task for you to fulfil from the heavens if you pay close attention. Most times it is not just by about winning souls, the more you search within yourself and reflect on the things that have happened, you will begin to attract souls of a similar vibration as they will be attracted by your light.

GIDEON E SAMSON'S ENCOUNTER WITH THE CREATOR... MARCH 31ST 2021

O n this day, I had an encounter with a green fire in my vision. I was stranded in a foreign country and broken, with no friends and no one I could trust. I had given up on the last person I had loved. I was filled with the word of God in my heart, but I had no one to share it with. I prayed in tears that night and slept outside next to the open sea, with my little black bag and Bible. I was frustrated and confused because I had recently resigned from a job that almost caused me to sin against God and my body (the temple of God). The pay and accommodation given from the job at that time was important because I was in a foreign country. I resigned from two jobs during this period. The scripture says if your left hand will try and make you sin against God and stop you from going to the kingdom of heaven, cut it off. On that night, in my weakness and tears, I dreamt and witnessed a green fire coming to me in my vision at 3am in the morning from above the sea. The green fire said to me: "since no one is your friend, I will be your friend'." Immediately, it left, and I subconsciously was gifted with the strength of a superhuman.

It was like I was falling into the sea in my dream, but I pulled myself back up and flew to another world. I entered a house through the rooftop and saw a woman and a baby, then I woke up. The frustrations I had included me thinking that the woman I married had tricked me, but it was all a test, from this world.

Before that day, I had been baptized a long time ago by other believers in a church, but after my revelation from the father, I walked up to the sea in that same morning and was rebaptized by the sea through the spirit of God. When I woke up that morning, I did not think, I just walked up and down the hill to the sea to get washed. I sat down on a little rock below and let the sea flow on me. My thoughts at that time were not functioning because it was still early. This was the first time I truly received the Holy Spirit and had no restrictions. Ever since then, I have received directions and communication from heaven through the Holy Spirit towards people and the world.

My heart was open to understanding everything beyond what my mind and eyes could not comprehend, and this made me not feel weak and alone anymore. I also don't feel part of the world or part of where I was from. I do not believe I came from there because we see far and beyond where we came from if we are truly awakened.

Why still trap yourself in a box of procrastination?

The Holy Spirit

T he Holy Spirit gives us a chance, after Jesus Christ, to speak to the universe and receive answers on our own. That is why it mostly looks like everyone is spiritual. This happens through faith alone. This is why this generation feels they are God or that God reflects through them. This feeling comes because of the Holy Spirit. Without the Holy Spirit, all the flesh produces are lust, hatred, unforgiveness, selfishness, greed and so on. All these names are not just feelings, they happen through experiences of the individual's life.

So many people question where they come from, circumstances surrounding their birth and growth, they blame God for putting them in that position. The first man born on Earth was not Adam but Cain and Abel.

Pain and struggling were recorded from them tilling and producing crops from the earth. As time went by, civilization came into existence and a system was created. People had to leave their homes to make money, which was implemented by the LEADERS long before now people had faith and hope on everything a leader in power says. The system created money and God created the entire world for us to enjoy living in comfort, which is supposed to be free. The devil does not have the same power he did before Jesus Christ.

Before Jesus Christ, there was a strict principle applied to knowing God, how he affects a person's life and how they receive blessings God has written these laws to function in the universe and everything else he has created we are made with purity, to have a solid relationship with God you must pass the test of purity and faithfulness.

The Earth principle, when it was controlled by the devil, brought people down out of principles from the spiritual laws that protect everything GOD has created in the Earth. He could punish men with sickness, people lost their lives and everything they had for no reason evil spirits and demons lived and tormented the bodies of humans, but after Christ, he was defeated and fallen.

The Earth experienced total peace after Jesus Christ's resurrection. We experience this peace until now. Only money makes us struggle here on Earth.

The devil has lost the power that he uses against men, so he created money. Because of money and pain, people make covenants with their blood, without that no one will think about giving their soul away. The scripture said you cannot serve God and serve money. The devil makes you confused towards life and he attracts you. In real life, the system created this confusion among men, if we do not pursue wealth the devil won't be able to convince people into making blood covenants. Sex is a blood covenant and can spiritually create a bond between you and a person. This is why the devil makes you sleep with multiple persons in secret meetings, so one's sense of purity of the Holy Spirit to the body dies. All that you will crave for is pleasure, this comes with a lot of ignorance, it builds pain as time goes, many of them end up taking their own life.

All these things are happening through our leaders today, they are the only way to the people right now, most of them help the devil in fulfilling his vision, without them the devil will remain powerless, because Jesus Christ of Nazareth has won him and set us free from his spiritual strength over us.

The reason sex is the devil's greatest weapon in bringing humans down is because sex opens the body of any individual, when we partake in unclean sex our body is then open and vulnerable without protection. When you have it with multiple people you defile your flesh, and this kills the consciousness. Of good and common sense that comes from your soul. Secret society, porn, music that worships your flesh, the system, all push pleasures, and desire to the flesh. When your body is defiled by sex, you have opened yourself to all the world has to offer (pleasure, pain, frustration, anger, pride, ego, selfishness). In return for it all is money.

If Daniel can trust God in the lion's den, you can trust God in your stresses and worries.

1. THE FLESH

I n the ancient tales of creation, the divine sculptor fashioned the clay of flesh, imbuing it with the breath of the divine.

Thus, the spirit of the Almighty flow through the sinews of the first being. Yet, when Adam beheld the shadow cast by his own self - the flesh - he lost his luster, and his glory faded. So it was that Adam glimpsed the duality of his nature, and the scripture tells this tale. It said the first thing Adam noticed was fear and weakness (nakedness). The flesh was created to become an image of the spirit of God, my thoughts are that God fell in love with his reflection and gave it life. Death is the reward for the flesh. Everything on Earth dies; it only existed on Earth and not from the Garden of Eden "God's secret place". The Earth was created for cultivation and exploration for the supernatural beings.

Adam was one of these because he was also created in a supernatural glory. Adam was given dominion over Earth and the universe. Everything that runs from the earth is controlled by Angels and they operate with the universe.

Angels are magical beings given different powers by God to operate the nature of the Earth. Most of the miracles performed in the bible before Jesus Christ was done by Angels. "I am sure Jesus Christ commanded the angels at the will of his father". The earth is alive and breathing. Everything grows from it except man-made creations. All looks dead as time hits it; it depreciates even in its beauty colour. Look at riches and wealth and all the gatherings of material possessions.

As time moved on men fell more to ignorance and forgot their reason for living. They started hating one another. This is the reason Jesus had to make a new decree on our behalf through his death. He defeated death because death could not bind him by the laws of the earth. He was not of the earth; he gave us back the spirit of God into our consciousness.

Without the spirit of God, we are simply the same as the animals and everything creeping throughout the earth, they exist, and they do not. The flesh without the spirit of God just demands for food and sex, and mostly the fear of death. They are short sighted and do not view anything else other than self and physical needs. The flesh has just two needs; hunger and pleasure. What to eat and what to enjoy? Let us check back on what Solomon said about life.

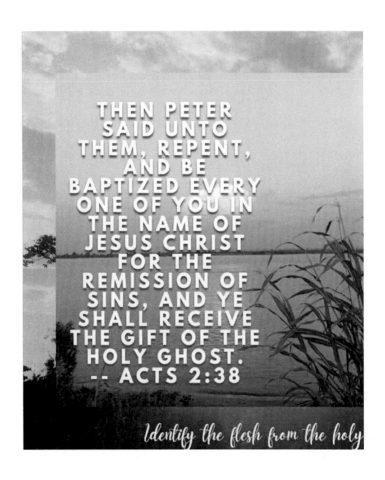

THEN PETER SAID UNTO THEM, REPENT, AND BE BAPTIZED EVERY ONE OF YOU IN THE NAME OF JESUS CHRIST FOR THE REMISSION OF SINS, AND YE SHALL RECEIVE THE GIFT OF THE HOLY GHOST. -- ACTS 2:38

Identify the flesh from the holy

2. ECCLESIASTES

All Is Vanity

The words of the Preacher, the son of David, king in Jerusalem. Vanity of vanities, says the Preacher, vanity of vanities! All is vanity. What does man gain by all the toil at which he toils under the sun? A generation goes, and a generation comes, but Earth remains forever. The sun rises and the sun goes down and hastens to the place where it rises. The wind blows to the south and goes around to the north; around and around goes the wind, and on its circuits the wind returns. All streams run to the sea, but the sea is not full; to the place where the streams flow, there they flow again. All things are full of weariness; A man cannot utter it; The eye is not satisfied with seeing, nor the ear filled with hearing. What has been what will be, and what has been done is what will be done, and there is nothing new under the sun. Is there a thing, of which it is said, "See, this is new"? It has been already in the ages before us. There is no remembrance of former things, nor will there be any remembrance of later things yet to be among those who come after.

3. THE VANITY OF WISDOM

I the Preacher have been king over Israel in Jerusalem.

I. And I applied my heart to seek and to search out by wisdom all that is done under heaven. It is an unhappy business that God has given to the children of man to be busy with.

II. I have seen everything that is done under the sun, and behold, all is vanity and a striving after wind. What is crooked cannot be made straight, and what is lacking cannot be counted. I said in my heart, "I have acquired great wisdom, surpassing all who were over Jerusalem before me, and my heart has had great experience of wisdom and knowledge."

III. And I applied my heart to know wisdom and to know madness and folly. I perceived that this also is but a striving after wind. For in much wisdom is much vexation, and he who increases knowledge increases sorrow.

4. THE VANITY OF SELF-INDULGENCE

I said in my heart, "Come now, I will test you with pleasure; enjoy yourself." But behold, this also was vanity. King Solomon's wisdom was from the flesh, but the wisdom of Jesus Christ is from the beginning before man was created.

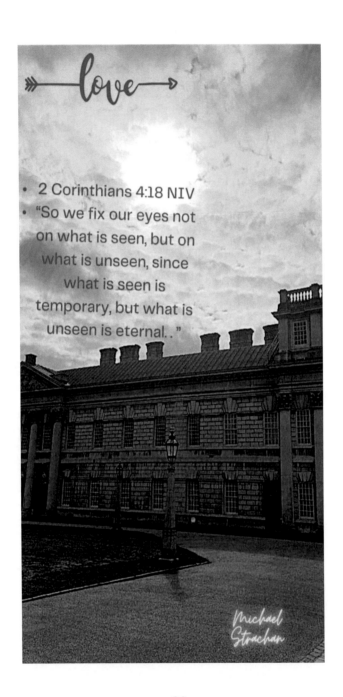

love

- 2 Corinthians 4:18 NIV
- "So we fix our eyes not on what is seen, but on what is unseen, since what is seen is temporary, but what is unseen is eternal. ."

Michael Strachan

5. FREE - WILL

The Concept of Sin and Righteousness in Christianity

According to Christian doctrine, sin exists on a deeper level than the commandments given during the time of Moses. Sin dates to the time of Adam and, as such, goes beyond mere obedience to God's laws. While obedience is essential, the core of Christianity is rooted in the concept of freewill. As the world evolved, the supernatural became less apparent. Thus, being a true believer is more about leading a supernatural life than it is about the knowledge of the Bible. True obedience, then, means reclaiming our freewill and achieving righteousness, as the scripture describes. This book will be meaningful to Bible scholars who approach it with an open mind. Jesus Christ is a central figure in Christian theology.

Before his death, Jesus was able to perform miracles and control the physical world. After his death, he attained righteousness, which allowed him to appear to more people at once. The apostle Paul had an encounter with the risen Jesus in physical form after his death.

Many believers, however, are still emotionally attached to Christianity and have yet to experience a true revelation of righteousness. Such a revelation brings a sense of enlightenment, inspiring one to carry the cross of Jesus Christ and live a true righteous life.

Adam had dominion over Earth from the Garden of Eden. There is a part through Earth that leads to the Garden of Eden. When Adam ate the tree of life, he lost his glory (separation from God's glory) afterwards he lost dominion over the earth. (Let me stop explaining the hidden secrets of the Bible we could do that forever if you are a firm believer).

Dominion is giving back to you by the Holy Spirit through Jesus, not as Adam had it, but this time with faith to pass the test of Good and evil. Before we receive our rewards, the Holy Spirit helps you to make your decrees about your life, to bless yourself, to encourage others and to do extraordinary things through prayers and faith. There is no limit to the free gifts God has for us. I access it in a unique way from others because I don't debate with sinful thoughts.

6. THE FUNCTIONS OF THE FLESH

The flesh lets us feel and desire. These feelings have led many astray. You can build this flesh as it is a weapon to be used for Christ Jesus but not for your feelings. The flesh has its own demands from the spirit. The flesh was not created to be alive on its own, but created to reflect a divine God and to do extraordinary things like he can through his spirit.

When Adam was cursed, he was cursed to till the ground which means before the curse he did not have to till the ground he had the authority of dominion through words like God towards the earth. After all was cast out from the garden God created cherubim and seraphim to guide the gates of the Garden of Eden and to stop Adam from coming back. When your flesh is alive without the spirit of God you pay more attention to pain and desire. Pain and desire belong to the Earth as short as life is, unfortunately, everything passes as fast as it has started.

7. THE GOOD REPORT STARTS WITH YOU!!!

GIDI
THE GOOD REPORT STARTS WITH YOUR THOUGHTS OVER THE SITUATION NOT THE REPORT FROM THE SITUATION ❤

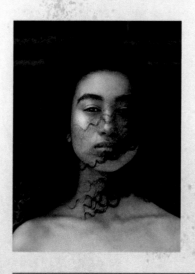

Take care of your soul first your body will meet up
@free from sin channels

8. DEVIL'S TRICK TO THE FLESH

We are indeed God's children created with love and emotions, not for suffering, but for the fullness of all things good. The flesh always shows the same feelings to all humans, as we are all one in heart and equal.

Pride
Jealousy
Set back thoughts
Rejection of oneself
Low self esteem
Wants
Ignorance
Unforgiveness

We can go on, but my point is you could blame all this on the devil because he invented it all, but you cannot always blame the devil for your ignorance towards the things that are good. All these things mentioned about the devil still falls on Emotions (lacking God's words). We will fall short and become a seed of darkness as every deed was first felt before putting to reality. This earth is a soil we plant and harvest from the ground the same is as actions are with reality. Actions are the seed; the earth takes this seed and plays the results for you the next day or some years later. Every day is a judgment day for the earth. The scripture says as long as the Earth remains seeded time and harvest shall not seize. We shall always reap what we sow, as humans, we were all born in one way and that is birth. When a baby is born the only thing that matters to the newborn is food, after this there is touch, care, and love. The newborn starts to differentiate character and makes meaning to what it sees and hears.

Twenty years later that baby is a grown adult. That soul is meant for possibilities if it is connected to God as it was in the beginning. This is where our lord Jesus Christ solved the puzzle of getting men back to God. "A new decree paid with a better sacrifice can rule over the formal decree and its formal sacrifices."

Since we cannot understand anything about the supernatural Jesus Christ of Nazareth has given the Holy Spirit to Earth again but not as before. This time to help you and your thoughts to righteousness and peace, without him you won't get through many challenges.

9. THE GLORIOUS BODY

J esus Christ of Nazareth preached in parables and performed miracles because he knew that the multitude would not understand what they can't see. He came from the highest realms to the flesh and remained aware. After his death, he attained righteousness. Only he walked with faith and holiness on Earth. Our glorious body is the spiritual state totally being in control of the physical state. Without restrictions of our flesh the spirit of God totally takes control of the flesh. Holiness is what we can strive for on Earth to carry the task of God and not our own. To do things because of God's plan, not for our wants. Jesus Christ wants us to be fishers of men not pleasers of men. The Holy Spirit does not function in perfection it functions in truth. Have you ever spoken to someone who hurt you so much? How did you feel? Keeping the truth from yourself hurts more than holding the truth back cursed blindness to your heart.

The Holy Spirit functions with truth and transparency. Truth frees your heart as you get older, you become happier and calmer. People who can't handle the truth are dealing with "Unforgiveness" and "Hate" towards their life experiences.

10. TIME

T ime was invented when the sun and moon were created. Time exists because of day and night. Time plays a long role in whatever we do on Earth both in secret and open. As soon as we wake up, we continue in our circle and start to drop at going back to bed, if you don't you will fall ill, as the earth is said to be spherical that's how human life goes on in a circle. The formal reality of man was not stuck on the earthly programming. We live beyond the activities of the universe; we were in control and had dominion over everything. Everyone on Earth is aware of their time, in less than 150 years almost 3 generations can die off. People die every day and babies being born every day and as time goes on, the world can change without anyone even noticing. The system is aware of this time on Earth and is making use of it well. Pause for a while and look around! You must have been doing the same thing again. Most people are stuck in idle thoughts it makes them desire their own bodies. Time is a seed, anything we think or do today is recorded as your reward for your tomorrow. As you sleep each day, the activities of that day have been recorded in you, when you wake up the next day you become your results of yesterday.

11. EPHESIANS 5-15

Therefore, be imitators of God, as beloved children. And walk in love, as Christ loved us and gave himself up for us, a fragrant offering and sacrifice to God.

But sexual immorality and all impurity or covetousness must not even be named among you, as is proper among saints.

Let there be no filthiness nor foolish talk nor crude joking, which are out of place, but instead let there be thanksgiving. For you may be sure of this, that everyone who is sexually immoral or impure, or who is covetous (that is, an idolater), has no inheritance in the kingdom of Christ and God.

Let no one deceives you with empty words, for because of these things the wrath of God comes upon the sons of disobedience. Therefore, do not become partners with them; for at one time, you were darkness, but now you are light in the Lord.

Walk as children of light (for the fruit of light is found in all that is good, right, and true) And try to discern what is pleasing to the Lord.

Take no part in the unfruitful works of darkness, but instead expose them.

For it is shameful even to speak of the things that they do in secret.

But when anything is exposed by the light, it becomes visible, for anything that becomes visible is light. Therefore, it says:

"Awake, Oh sleeper, and arise from the dead, and Christ will shine on you."

Look carefully then how you walk, not as unwise but as wise.

Making the best use of the time because the days are evil.

Therefore, do not be foolish, but understand what the will of the Lord is. And do not get drunk with wine, for that is debauchery, but be filled with the Spirit.

Addressing one another in psalms and hymns and spiritual songs, singing and making melody to the Lord with your heart. Giving thanks always and for everything to God the Father in the name of our Lord Jesus Christ, submitting to one another out of reverence for Christ.

12. GRACE

Grace in Christian theology is the spontaneous un-merited gift of the divine favor in the salvation of sinners, and the divine influence operating in individuals for their regeneration and sanctification to function in grace, you must be aware of the choices you make. Those who are disobedience function with grace from a savings point, those who are obedient function in grace with power and miracles. Grace gives us a lot of chances to repent and change before we die of this earth, the principal of grace only last if you live in this earth after death what you sow is what you will reap and what you don't repent from will become your demon in hell. Grace with a holy life is where you activate the supernatural life of the spirit of God in your flesh.

Your flesh becomes more timid and humbler if you deprive it from its wants. You see how people who have everything feel the need to talk with pride in them because they think it helps them live without restrictions. The grace to live is the most beautiful gifts on earth though others are living so painful, and many are disabled life has always been that way, but everything showed in others is to make us aware of the differences of life around us.

The feelings of the flesh can make you become ungrateful and view yourself as a God above others especially when you are successful. The reason most elites will not make it to heaven is because their results and substance made them rely on their words and not God's words. They gradually slide backwards from their faith and stand by the strength of the world.

Romans 3:24: "[We] are justified by his grace as a gift, through the redemption that is in Christ Jesus." Grace is what inclines God to give gifts that are free and undeserved by sinners.

Romans 5:15: "If many died through one man's trespass, much more have the grace of God and the free gift by the grace of that one-man Jesus Christ abounded for many." So, grace is that quality in God that produces free gifts for guilty sinners in salvation.

Romans 11:5–6: "At the present time there is a remnant, chosen by grace. But if it is by grace, it is no longer based on works; otherwise, grace would no longer be grace." So, you can't work to earn grace. It is free and undeserved.

Corinthians 12:9: "My grace is sufficient for you, for my power is made perfect in weakness."

Corinthians 15:10: 'But by the grace of God I am what I am, and his grace toward me was not in vain. On the contrary, I worked harder than any of them, though it was not I, but the grace is a gift, and every gift is giving so you can use it, knowing you acquire the grace of God does not mean you should be careless and undisciplined because our actions even with all the grace of God around us will create a certain reality for us. Most times we go through experiences because of our actions ignorant realties have been created by us, we wanted to partake in

them, does the grace of God still speak for this ignorance... yes!

The grace of God does not take you back in time to fix
our mistakes, but it helps you heal and realize through
your actions and choices after repentance.

13. FAITH WORKS WITH OBEDIENCE

*F*aith was not designed for you to archive material substances on Earth; you were not designed for that purpose. This generation has lost touch of God because most think God as only a blessing giver and only place demand on him.

14. HEBREW 11:1

Faith is for a spiritual journey; along that journey, if you are constantly obedient, you will find God's provision. Many people talk about faith in the wrong direction, for example, people have faith towards getting a house or a car, some towards recovering from an illness. These things are not what faith is designed for; faith was designed for the vision of God's calling in your life, because as righteousness allows, we live beyond the activities of the earth problems. Once you are obedient to God's mission, what many suffer from will be your testimony. Faith is designed for the mission of God's words; you cannot function in faith without knowing your calling. Jesus Christ of Nazareth had faith in his calling along with his obedience to his calling; on his journey, he experienced the provision and miracles that took place from the father (God).

Hebrews 11:15-20

15. It was by faith that even Sarah was able to have a child, though she was barren and was too old. She believed that God would keep his promise.

16. And so, a whole nation came from this one man who was as good as dead—a nation with so many people that, like the stars in the sky and the sand on the seashore, there is no way to count them.

17. All these people died still believing what God had promised them. They did not receive what was promised, but they saw it all from a distance and welcomed it. They

agreed that they were foreigners and nomads here on Earth.

18. Obviously, people who say such things are looking forward to a country they can call their own.

19. If they had longed for the country they came from, they could have gone back.

20. But they were looking for a better place, a heavenly homeland. That is why God is not ashamed to be called their God, for he has prepared a city for them.

James 4:2-3

2. You desire but do not have, so you kill. You covet but you cannot get what you want, so you quarrel and fight. You do not have because you do not ask God.

3. When you ask, you do not receive, because you ask with wrong motives, that you may spend what you get on your pleasures.

HOLY SPIRIT

15. The Holy Spirit

T he Holy Spirit is the reflection of Christ and his character. It is also the spirit of God and without the Holy Spirit a man's heart is focused on the things of the earth. The spirit of God helps to see beyond the present and to see life beyond death. "Death" should not be seen from just life and death. It is simply about the earthly pains, regrets, hungers, depressions, and these are the things Christ has come to redeem us from. The Holy Spirit is the spirit of God given back to men to direct us to righteousness. Righteousness is a supernatural state and no man on Earth is righteous yet. You only love God here and show holiness. Righteousness is the destination of our soul; we are still in the race. The Holy Spirit is a gift from our Lord Jesus Christ after his death. Can a person have a good heart without the Holy Spirit? Yes. This is because people are born with free will and most people find themselves good-hearted from birth, we only reflect the behaviour of our upbringing. A lot of people reflect this as they get older. Those that want change should make it happen.

Humans tend to reflect the character that suits their flesh. When you read the word of God and act accordingly to its principles and directions righteousness begins to reflect through your flesh before your death day.

This will make you look, act, and talk different from the rest of humanity. The things of the earth come with troubles and worries but the Holy Spirit keeps you peaceful and this peace reveals the vision of God to your soul. Everyone is equipped with different unique gifts from the

Holy Spirit and if we understand that the things we desire and keep within us reflect through the flesh. We try to hide our desires, but we act, talk and become like what we do or desire. Only people who are short sighted can easily be deceived by the things they behold. The flesh has its reward every day. Do you not know that your bodies are temples of the Holy Spirit, who is in you, whom you have received from God? You are not your own; you were bought at a price. Therefore, honour God with your bodies.

16. HOW CAN WE GROW THE HOLY SPIRIT IN US?

1 Corinthians 6:19-20
But the Advocate, the Holy Spirit, whom the Father will send in my name, will teach you all things and will remind you of everything I have said to you.

John 14:26
They saw tongues of fire that separated and came to rest on each of them. All of them were filled with the Holy Spirit and began to speak in other tongues as the Spirit enabled them.

Acts 2:3-4
Therefore, go and make disciples of all nations, baptizing them in the name of the Father and of the Son and of the Holy Spirit, and teaching them to obey everything I have commanded you. And surely, I am with you always, to the very end of the age.

Matthew 28:19-2
On hearing this, they were baptized in the name of the Lord Jesus. When Paul placed his hands on them, the Holy Spirit came on them, and they spoke in tongues and prophesied.

Acts 19:5-6
After being born again you will receive the Holy Spirit from Jesus Christ in faith your body will be equipped with light and peace, the experience is magical and healing, though at first it comes with lots of tests, but if you endure and prove your desires for purity too be true you will experience great things happening.

It's amazing because even if things look bad you will have endless peace flowing through your heart, always speak out and let your worries out don't stuff thoughts in yourself, many times when we are surrounded by good listeners and good friends, we find healing from the things that border our soul, only people who know God's love can fully understand and through this connection to our heavenly father we are able to heal anyone.

17. DEEDS AND THE WORD OF GOD AWAKENS ALL THE BRIGHT ENERGIES THAT COMES WITH THE SPIRIT OF GOD

18. LOVE IS THE EMOTIONAL PART OF GOD WHICH IS HIS FIRST-BORN JESUS CHRIST OF NAZARETH

God is love; love is not a word but a spirit that came as a person at God's time. Jesus Christ represented himself as love and gave us the final commandment which is to "Love our neighbours as ourselves and love God with all your heart". Love is a living spirit and only Jesus Christ came to represent love. Love from the earth mostly depends on expectations and needs, love from above stands alone and gives alone...

Love is the son of God, if we think love is a feelings we have fallen short to the Earth... feelings have a lot to do with our wants from our bodies, God should be the foundation of any relationship or marriage if you want it too last, love is Jesus Christ and understanding comes from within the Holy Spirit, the human body is never satisfied it takes God to fill. The soul, Genesis 1. Then God said, "Let us make mankind in our image, in our likeness, so that they may rule over the fish in the sea and the birds in the sky, over the livestock and all the wild animals, and over all the creatures that move along the ground."

So, God created mankind in his own image, in the image of God he created them; Jesus Christ was there when the world was created, he was one of us God referred too, nothing that witnessed the creation can be consumed by it. Jesus Christ gave his life to be killed in time, so he can save those that are lost there. Without the soul time we would be useless, this makes your soul your time.

The Devil and the Earth's Mysteries

The Devil is believed to be in pursuit of our souls, and upon obtaining them, he will offer the earth as a reward. The universe is a powerful place, and it was created for us to explore. Our thoughts can influence and react to nature in a unique way. Each person lives in their own universe because the reality of life only becomes apparent after death. Perhaps King Solomon was trying to say that even wisdom and foolishness are meaningless. Supernatural beings in the Bible lose their way on Earth because they don't have free will like humans do. Only upon coming to Earth can they live freely. While the lifespan of humans is limited, most alien blood is believed to be immortal. Everything we see around us, from the sun and the moon to the rain and animals, is a part of the Earth's beauty and mysteries.

The Purpose of Nature and Our Perception of Wealth

It's easy to believe that nature exists solely for our benefit and comfort. However, without this system, there would be no concept of wealth or poverty. While we often rely on the government to provide our needs, the reality is that the earth provides everything we require. Isn't it interesting that we spend money on gold, which derives from the earth, only to craft it into images and worship it?

19. 1 CORINTHIANS 13

But if I have no love, I am nothing.

3 I may give away everything I have, and even give up my body to be burned — but if I have no love, this does me no good.

4 Love is patient and kind; it is not jealous or conceited or proud;

5 Love is not ill-mannered or selfish or irritable; love does not keep a record of wrongs;

6 Love is not happy with evil, but is happy with the truth.

7 Love never gives up; and its faith, hope, and patience never fail.

8 Love is eternal. There are inspired messages, but they are temporary; there are gifts of speaking in strange tongues, but they will cease; there is knowledge, but it will pass.

9 for our gifts of knowledge and of inspired messages are only partial;

10 but when what is perfect comes, then what is partial will disappear.

11 When I was a child, my speech, feelings, and thinking were all those of a child; now that I am an adult, I have no more use for childish ways.

12 What we see now is like a dim image in a mirror; then we shall see face-to-face. What I know now is only partial; then it will be complete—as complete as god's knowledge of me.

13 Meanwhile these three remain: faith, hope, and love; and the greatest of these is love, judgement is for God.

-1 Corinthians 15:58
Therefore, my beloved brothers, be steadfast, immovable, always abounding in the work of the Lord, knowing that in the Lord your labor is not in vain.

20. JUDGEMENT

Judgement

IDENTIFY THE FLESH FROM THE HOLY SPIRIT

Any man who judges blinds themselves from being aware of their flaws. Judgement and correction are not the same. Correction exists because of love and not judgment. Anyone who judges cannot correct they only condemns and gossip. My dear beloved brothers and sisters stop being judgmental, it makes you look foolish before God and yourself. God is the only judge because he alone sees the secret and heart of every soul.

Apart from God who are we to put labels on anyone, everyone has different part, and each part produces unique experience. We can only love and understand each other being judgmental has made a lot of people hide their sin and anything kept in secret becomes a master of you. Choose what to keep and what to release.

21. BAPTISM

By Gideon E Samson

Baptism from my point of view has been born out of water and not out of flesh. Jesus said to John The Baptist:

"Let it be so now; it is proper for us to do this to fulfil all righteousness." Then John consented.

Just as the new principle of righteousness overcame the old principle of sin, this is the new principle of water baptism by the spirit, which overcomes the principle of the earth which is been born by the flesh. Anyone born by the flesh will believe and see only the things of the flesh. The flesh is limited by many laws of the earth, but the spirit of God quickens the flesh to overcome this law through the grace of our lord Jesus Christ.

Holiness is for you to make yourself available for the will of God, it is extremely important to abstain yourself from sin. Please clear your heart and be expressional, the devil's strength is in accusations, if you are faulty, you will be restricted.

The world will become your enemy when you listen to the word of God and abstain yourself from unclean activities your body which has become God's temple.

When you listen to God's word you will be given the spirit gift when approved. Look at your life from the beginning is it in line with the word of God (look back on

your life experience and navigate through the way you live if you have been living the life designed for you by GOD OR YOU LIVED THE LIFE DESIGN BY THE FLESH), these are important words to help heal the hearts and minds of everyone here on Earth.
Amen.

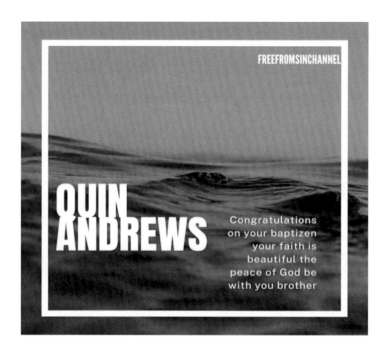

FREEFROMSINCHANNEL

QUIN
ANDREWS

Congratulations
on your baptizen
your faith is
beautiful the
peace of God be
with you brother

Baptism story by Qyntavius Andrews

B efore my baptism I was unsure of love. I felt often
confused by the wisdoms of gurus, spiritual teach-
ers, and the bible itself. I had studied mythologies
from all over the globe since 2012 and continue to study
them. Indian mythology was what I had invested much
time in understanding.

Due to nonduality and new spiritual movements connected to Buddhism and Vedic mysticism I had studied
many ancient texts in connection to the Indian spiritual
science and philosophies. I grew up with a Christian family but no one in my family took the time to really help
me understand it more deeply.

So, I grew resentful towards the indoctrinated ideology of the common Christian or any religious movements because the surface understanding is not what helps me understand things. I enjoy when someone can take small steps and really sit down with me to point out every nuance thing as it leads to deeper and broader constructs and understandings. During these years of study and practice I had learned ideas of no rules. No consequences. So, I practiced all things immoral and only viewed Spirituality through the desire for Happiness and Sexual Bonding. I feel that I am just one of many who are led astray by similar experiences and this testimony can help others see a way out of the confusion or the following of harmful information when searching for answers to Spiritual Nurturing.

In the end there is much I am unaware of. Gidi Samson helped me with my life and my integrity in such a profound way. I am grateful for him because I have reestablished my power, ability, faculty of purpose and desire for living. I learned that I have potential and gifts to give to others to help myself and others through the light and grace of God. May you be blessed as Christ has blessed me.

Amen

WELCOMES MICHAEL STRACHAN

Congratulations on your baptizen your faith is beautiful ,the peace of God be with you amen

Baptism story by Michael Strachan

Before being baptised by Gideon Samson and receiving the Holy Spirit in March 2023 I had many uncomfortable experiences since I was a kid and experienced some traumatic events which had a great impact on me into my adult life. I felt like no one understood me or my intentions growing up which included my family, friends, work colleagues and people I met throughout my life. I knew from a noticeably young that the world was strange, and people acted crazy. I always wondered why my family had so many challenges and I could not understand why some people had an abundance of wealth, multiple homes and many were homeless, waterless, and foodless. It seemed illogical to me and strange that people in society accepted this way of living as being normal.

I grew up being shown about Yeshua (Jesus) and the bible through different sources but due to the damage I had seen in the world, religion had been used to justify the crusades, inquisition and many more holy wars which made me think that religion was the root cause of problems in the world today. I thought if something is holy then why I thought do we do not have peace and harmony in the world and why are there always wars in the name of religions?

I was in a lot of pain and was suffering for a long time and I felt broken at how people treated each other in the world. I could see that many did not care about the well-being of others and only focussed on themselves, and this seemed inhumane to me. I also saw that many religious people were not following the words of our heavenly father/Yeshua (Jesus) and their actions did not reflect their words.

Also, to my horror I found out that many ungodly acts were being committed in the world and the ones in power on this Earth worshipped the devil it seemed and were incredibly open about it. This made me feel alone and I questioned our heavenly father about why the inhumanity exists in this world. I realised that the inhumanity in the world was not our creators doing and life was being influenced from the spirit realms.

I was shown signs about future events to come and tried to warn friends and family, but I was met with reactions I did not expect, I was hurt and felt alone and knew that there were global events on their way that would affect the whole planet. I then started to distance myself from my friends and family as no one understood me or my concerns. I tried to warn my family about the dangers of taking vaccines, I always thought that you could share your experiences and people would listen and learn from one another, but I received a big shock.

Then one day through amazing circumstances (no such thing as coincidences in this world), I was really hurting emotionally, and I prayed to our heavenly father to help guide me and show me the truth after receiving many revelations about this world.

Then within a brief period "miracles" occurred; a random event led me to meet someone in a store who told me about people marching in London against the pandemic amongst many more inhumane things happening in the world. I joined many online groups around injustice, spirituality and against the lock downs, forced vaccinations (especially against kids), whilst many people lost their jobs, homes, marriages, and relationships during the pandemic, but this was not highlighted in the media. Despite the fact it felt like the world was ending but it was also a great opportunity for the unseen things to become seen and a blessing to all those that were looking to find answers about our purpose here on Earth.

Many people spent more time with their families, people started up their own businesses, but it wasn't like that for everyone. I spoke with many homeless people that simply lost everything and had no support from the system. I experienced traumatic experiences trying to get support from the system i.e. Doctors, hospitals, police, government, and solicitors, only to find out the whole system was corrupt, and it wasn't about uplifting people with love, compassion, wisdom (our creators) and integrity. It was about controlling the masses through Tele LIE vison to disconnect us from our creator and his holy son Yeshua.

During the pandemic, a woman I met in one of these online groups I was introduced to told me that she had a NDE (near death experience) and explained all that happened to her when she died and where she went. She said she was met by millions of spirits all watching her life on a big screen, they were reviewing her life told that her role was not finished yet and she was sent back. She explained that a sign that said infinite landed on her head and before that she was listening to a song with lyrics that pre-warned her of this upcoming out of body experience. She was in a coma for several months and I then saw that all this was true because she was on the BBC news sharing this same story and involved in a dispute, so all her words were validated. I knew what she said was true because I cried when she told me, I always knew deep down that we never died and that was one of the greatest deceptions we are told from birth. The biggest validation was that I prayed with all my heart days before to our creator that I wanted to know the truth about why we are here and why inhumanity exists. My prayers were answered...

It is difficult to explain but my energy heightens when I hear the truth being spoken. The truth has already been written in our hearts so when I hear the words I can tell if what is being spoken about is truth or a lie. We have been blessed with intuition as we can hear our fathers voice if we listen carefully.

I joined the Spiritual groups and was surprised to see the division in groups that were meant to be united in standing up for our rights as God's children.

During this time, I created a group just to share my experiences but was flooded with other spiritual groups/information. Something within me said something was not right and I felt the truth is likely amazingly simple and all the information seemed to be over complicated purposely.

I reached a point in my life where I wanted to know the truth of our purpose here on Earth. I wanted to know why so much suffering existed in the world and why immoral people seemed to benefit financially.

I was going to marches in London and met my new girlfriend (who became my girlfriend later), we had a fun and carefree relationship where I finally met someone who seemed kind, caring and was actively standing up against corruption, before I joined a corrupt corporation (after just leaving one for the same reasons) everything started to change.

I was made homeless during the pandemic but for the grace of God I went through some amazing circumstances which resulted in me being rehoused in a beautiful area.

I started to become severely ill because of stressful experiences with work, housing and due to my spiritual practices, I found out. I realised that my ill health was a warning from my spirit that all was not well.

I have always been targeted wherever I went as I was always stood up for what was right and challenged authority wherever I went because I always believed that all our actions mattered, and we had to stand up against corruption and evil doing.

This happened at practically every job, and I just could not understand why people were trying to ruin my reputation until I gained more spiritual insights.

I developed conditions like IBS/Chrones disease, and the pain/uncomfortableness was something I have never experienced, and it lasted around 8 months. I knew deep down I was dying each day, and I could not understand why this was happening. I soon discovered that this was a spiritual attack and I only healed because I was shown a book that explained the root causes of disease, I learned more about emotions and understood that there are spirits which manipulate our thinking and health. The more we sin, the more we are open to these spiritual forces.

I had only at my job a month but knew from the beginning everyone was out for themselves. I tried to uplift and help people to make the right decisions (like most of my jobs) but everyone's intentions were different. They deliberately teamed up to get my out the company and sabotaged my accounts with big companies that would have helped many people find work. I was frustrated and angry and couldn't understand why I was experiencing the same challenges, because of these emotions I was holding onto it poisoned my body. It was made worse as no one knew the pain I was in and contributed to it.

I lost my girlfriend, home, job, finances, and lots of friends but it was all a blessing during this period of illness, I learned so much from these experiences.

But then I met someone who really made a positive impact in my life, his name is Qyntavius Andrews (story of his baptism in this book) in one of the spiritual groups and we connected instantly, we found each other though sharing pictures of our hands. We discussed the spiritual meaning of our hand patterns, we noticed we had the same mark on our hands (M) and that lead to many more spiritual conversations.

I was trying to control my reality and the outcomes of my actions, I realised I had to start letting go of the expectations and outcomes in my life and put my faith in our heavenly father, I started to heal (I have never looked back since).

I then fell into spiritual practice techniques like meditation, law of attraction, astrology and realised that something was not right, I discovered through conversations with my spiritual brother Qyntavius in the groups that most of what was being shared that was not about our heavenly father or Yeshua (Jesus) was actually Satanic doctrine like "new age religion" which focussed on things like law of attraction and that we are the creators of our reality (which is an abomination according to the word of our heavenly father). The issue with these spiritual practices is that our creator has a plan for us in our lives and if we focus on Earthly things like attracting wealth, we miss out on the great prize. A prize that is worth more than all the silver, gold, houses, holidays, careers this world has to offer.

Through our conversations we learned so much from one another. During my time of sickness Qyntavius really helped me heal, I was able to reduce my illness and physical pains and I realised it was because of my actions I was healing. I knew that our heavenly father sent Qyntavius and another person during this period to help lift me as my girlfriend left me during this time whilst I was ill, and it really would have been more devastating, but I felt lifted because I was starting to get more answers each day to my purpose here on Earth.

Through discussions with Qyntavius, we were able to learn from one another to grow spiritually and I was able to heal my sickness and remove certain beliefs that were not beneficial to me.

We are always growing and knew that everything is temporary. I learned that my journey was teaching me about solitude (letting go of attachments) and that my happiness is not dependant on another physical being or material objects. There was something so much more…Yeshua (Jesus) of Nazareth.

Qyntavius introduced me to Gideon, and everything changed instantly. Gideon told us truth that no one could know, and he was able to communicate with unconditional love the truth about our purpose here on Earth and about our heavenly father and his holy son Yeshua/Jesus Christ of Nazareth, he taught me about his values and what he did for humanity. The teachings have been hidden in this current maze of spiritual confusion.

This book is a blessing from our creator to tell people the "simple" truth about our heavenly father, sharing our testimonies showing everyone how much he loves us and how sin causes us pain in life. I was always frustrated in life that people did not think like me, so I kept moving and meeting new people always searching for true genuine souls who had similar spiritual experiences and I finally found them in Gideon and Qyntavius.

I was told things that only our creator would know about me, so I know with all my heart we are doing God's work. Gideon has similar experiences/abilities and sees the same signs and wonders as me, so I knew our heavenly father had brought him into my life for a reason.

I started to see more signs in my environment that would mirror either what I was thinking or gave me validation that the actions I was taking were approved by our father.

All the signs and messages, I am shown by the creator helped make me understand that we are all protected if we have faith in him and obedient to his will. I was permanently being targeted all my life and since being baptised everything changed for the better. I understood through reading the bible that there is no book that explains our existence in any better way.

I was only able to start understanding the bible after being baptised and I received the gift of speaking in tongues which I could have never imagined a few years ago. I have learnt there is a purpose for everyone, and anyone can have a personal relationship with our heavenly father.

I had spoken with Qyn and Gideon about wanting to prepare for my baptism in similar fashion to Qyn. I wanted to fully understand why Jesus was baptised and what it truly meant.

I was helped by my brothers, so I prepared for 2 days before maintaining my inner peace. I asked my house mate at the time if he would like to be my witness and he agreed gracefully. When I got baptised, I instantly felt different.

I was told before about how I would feel, and it was an amazing feeling and that this was the only thing missing in my life, I had to be reborn a new and I instantly I felt peace that I had never experienced before. I knew that this was what I had been searching for my whole life.

I realised that spiritual forces were manipulating me to keep me away from my path. When I came out of that water, I felt a profound sense of harmony I had not experienced before. It felt like for the first time all the noise had gone, and my clarity, wisdom and intuition developed rapidly.

Since my baptism my energy levels have changed, I am more focussed, less distracted and I even look a lot younger now since. Since gaining the Holy Spirit I feel directed daily, and it is an amazing feeling. I finally found our fathers grace along with my inner peace and harmony. I no longer suffer from depression, confusion, or direction. No matter what is thrown at me I have faith that everything is for our benefit and there is a right and wrong.

I discovered my life's purpose; I no longer suffer from my emotions like I did, and I feel blessed every day I wake up.

I only wish to honour our heavenly father through my actions now since being saved. To know our heavenly father and feel his presence we must be pure and have a child like heart.

Just before and after being baptised I started having encounters with angelic beings that would tell me messages. I met angels who were staring and pointing at a rainbow as I went to walk past them, they made me notice the rainbow and then we walked together, and I knew they were different to normal people. I also met either an angel or our heavenly father in human form, they that told me that I would change the world, the exact same words I said to my mum on the phone before this event.

Life is truly a blessing, and I can look back on all the traumatic, painful events in my life made me the person that I am. Our heavenly father loves us very much and I only wish to be of service to him and all my brothers and sisters.

Through the love of Jesus Christ and my brothers and sisters I was able to heal my wounds and I prayed to our father and repented for all the hurt I caused anyone (including thoughts I had against myself) and forgave those that hurt me. I felt a huge ten tonne weight being lifted off my back. I was able to rid myself of all addictions which are spirits of bondage. I discovered that many are being manipulated by spirits without realising.

14. For many are called, but few are chosen.

Concerning Spiritual Gifts

1 Corinthians 12
12. Now about the gifts of the Spirit, brothers, and sisters, I do not want you to be uninformed.

2. You know that when you were pagans, somehow or other you were influenced and led astray to mute idols.

3. Therefore I want you to know that no one who is speaking by the Spirit of God says, "Jesus be cursed," and no one can say, "Jesus is Lord," except by the Holy Spirit.

4. There are different kinds of gifts, but the same Spirit distributes them.

5. There are different kinds of service, but the same Lord.

6. There are different kinds of working, but in all of them and in everyone it is the same God at work.

7. Now to each one the manifestation of the Spirit is given for the common good.

8. To one there is given through the Spirit a message of wisdom, to another a message of knowledge by means of the same Spirit.

9. To another faith by the same Spirit, to another gifts of healing by that one Spirit.

10. To another miraculous powers, to another prophecy, to another distinguishing between spirits, to another speaking in different kinds of tongues.

11. All these are the work of one and the same spirit, and he distributes them to each one, just as he determines.

Ephesians 6:12
12. For we wrestle not against flesh and blood, but against principalities, against powers, against the rulers of the darkness of this world, against spiritual wickedness in high places.

The devil uses our flesh against us and seduces us with pleasures that end up making us feel empty and unloved. If we only focus on the material aspect of living, then we will truly never understand our purpose here on Earth. No matter how much material wealth and power you possess in this world, if it's not to be used for the benefit of our heavenly father than it is all simply vanity. We are daily fighting against our flesh and the temptations that come along with it.

It is time to create relationships that are transparent, empathetic, patient, loving and collaborative which follow the body of Christ. We are all members but with different functions (gifts). We are meant to uplift one another and make up for each other's weaknesses.

I see a lot of people with the spirit of pride in them and if they would just pray and ask father to help them with their purpose here on Earth, he would gladly assist. Our lives are more than our careers, our material possessions, and the holidays we go on.

It's time we created a more fruitful abundant planet that values the small things…Being kind, compassionate, caring and loving to everyone you meet. We must learn to love each other like our heavenly father. Only he can judge our hearts, thoughts, and actions as he sees all things. That doesn't mean we accept wrongdoing; we should always stand for truth in this world of lies and share our experiences and be transparent with one another. We were never meant to do this alone; we were meant to live together as one spirit.

It was never easy getting to his point, but I can now look forward with great hope.

Love thy neighbour as thyself and love our heavenly father with all your heart and you will see your life transform.

I am a testimony that our heavenly father and Yeshua is real as I didn't believe in the bible, Yeshua or thought a just creator oversaw this world but through hundreds and thousands of spiritual experiences and rapid growth after putting my faith in our father, especially since being Baptised with the Holy Spirit I am a now more balanced, blissful, spiritually aware child of God.

All praise to our father in the heavens and our Lord and saviour Yeshua of Nazareth... I will share my full testimony in time, and I only pray many others do the same.

Amen

After speaking with Qyntavius and Gideon Samson I prepared myself for a couple of days thinking about why Christ himself was baptized and maintained my inner peace whilst studying. I placed pictures and old memories around my bathroom, then I filled up the bath up to the top and I added Himalayan salt to the water, and I prayed upon the water with Apostle Gideon Samson as instructed. Then I submerged myself and after a few seconds came out of the water feeling completely different. I finally felt at peace x.

BEFORE BAPTISM

AFTER BAPTISM

WELCOMES OLIVIA SAMSON

Congratulations on your baptizen your faith is beautiful sister ,the peace of God be with you amen

Baptism story by Olivia Samson

Before my baptism, I had lived in the flesh, I never admitted I was wrong, suffered from pride and ego, hated been corrected and always held on to the wrong people had done to me. I never saw the efforts and love been showed to me It affected my relationship with everyone around me, I watched pornography and masturbated...I was born into a family which I knew had been chained by our ancestors and I really struggled to break free and possess a positive attitude.

My parents had brought I and my siblings up to go to church and read the scriptures, which I got tired of, not because I didn't love God or felt him in my heart and life, but because the church had lots of competitions, standard, gossips and sin, all this made me sad, and I started drifting from going to church. My parents got lost due to the hustle of the world, I slowly lost connections with them. I had known Gideon Samson from a very early stage in my life, although our relationship wasn't all perfect, I had watched and seen his endless heart and sacrifice towards everyone he came in contact with, he had good heart and intentions for everyone equally. I didn't understand our journey at those times and lived totally in the flesh, he was an Angel God had sent my way to love and correct me through this early part, he told me about his dreams and some revelations he had, and the meanings and our relationship was going to be more in my control and choices. It all started during the Covid, it was a total lockdown, we went apart for a long time, he was all alone in a state that had no light in 6 years, it wasn't a pretty experience, with no food or resources for this period because it came unexpectedly. Many months past and I missed him, I decided one night to leave my parents and go see him. When I got to Gidi he was more grown in the spirit and had a group where he taught and inspired people to live a good life.

He had been more grinded in the spirit and asked higher questions trying to understand what was really happening in the world.

He told me he had studied the bible many times with the light from the moon on empty stomach for days, and he noticed scriptures in the New Testament about Apostle Paul, he had certain understanding about mysteries from the scripture.

After the Covid, we got married, Gidi told me God had something great for him the next year and he could feel it in his spirit, the revelations and dreams he had started to come true, I was unaware of this times and didn't fight for our relationship like I should have, I choose my parents over him and didn't realize the damage it cost in his heart. Gidi and I separated for 4 months, in this month he travelled to a different country, he was tired of all the rejections and betrayal's he had been through. Because of my selfishness, I never could really see he was going through pain and challenges, I was lost in my emotions and had not taken charge at all, the revelation was happening, but I was blind, just as he had seen. Despite my Actions, I found out I was pregnant with my daughter, I told him about it, and he came back.

We went through some many process and different experiences, I had told him during our travels that some places we were was for me to learn, be patient with people and kill my ego and pride, because it had almost cost our marriage.

God showed us miracles in ways I can't explain, A new family that love and supported Gidi after our marriage, all through our challenging moment, the trust and love they had for him and our family was God's sent.

As it's said God takes us through experiences to prepare us for what's to come, we started travelling and been in different places at times that those people we went to really needed an Angel, it was in one of our journey's, on one faithful morning, Gidi entered into the room, I was and said there is a veil he sees in me, he asked me to take extra cloth and follow him. When we got to the river, he prayed, while he prayed, I taught about my past life, mistakes, flaws, I couldn't help but feel a lot of sorrow in my heart, I surrendered to God to just make me better. He went into the river and I went into, he held me and dipped me into the water, as a came out with faith and hope in me, I felt refreshed and muted. All my thoughts, worries, problems, paused. My transformation had started.

With time I grew, been baptized didn't stop me from feeling the way I used to, but it sharpened my intuition with time, to be able to see myself, my flaws, my lifestyle, my past, what I should have done better, what I should be doing better, the people around me, my level of awareness and balance, where I should be in my relationship with God and I saw I was ungrateful.

I started to ask more better questions, be more active and this had made me more happy from within. I have felt connected to my soul and can feel it. I have grown to recognize the holy spirit within me and connect to the fire and gift of the spirit.

This growth with God has become what I can't do without, when faced with choices am able to pause my reality, notice intentions and make right choices. This honestly wasn't what I use to be. I thank God for the opportunity to meet his son and be part of this testimony.

Amen

22. RAINBOW COVENANT

Genesis 9:12-17

A nd God said, "This is the sign of the covenant that I make between me and you and every living creature that is with you, for all future generations: I have set my bow in the cloud, and it shall be a sign of the covenant between me and the earth. When I bring clouds over the earth and the bow is seen in the clouds, I will remember my covenant that is between me and you and every living creature of all flesh. And the waters shall never again become a flood to destroy all flesh. When the bow is in the clouds, I will see it and remember the everlasting covenant between God and every living creature of all flesh that is on the Earth." God said to Noah, "This is the sign of the covenant that I have established between me and all flesh that is on the Earth."

L ike the appearance of a rainbow in a cloud on a rainy day, so was the appearance of the brightness all around it. This was the appearance of the likeness of the glory of the Lord" (Ezekiel 1:28).

T he Crown of Christ
Jesus, Through His work of redemption, was crowned with a sign of the Covenant of Grace (rainbow).

R evelation 10:1
I saw another strong angel coming down out of heaven, clothed with a cloud; and the rainbow was upon his head, and his face was like the sun, and his feet like pillars of fire.

23. GIDEON, FAMILY & FRIENDS

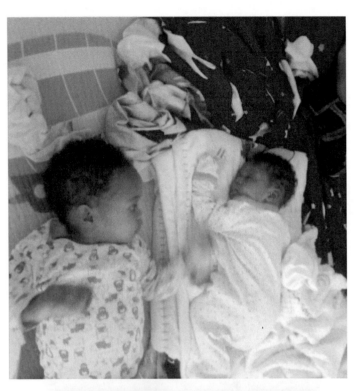

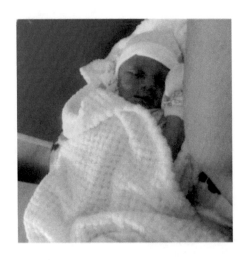

T his is the river that Gideon Samson baptized Olivia Samson and fellow brothers. Afterwards, a bright light of cloud came apon the river that evening.

After Gideon left that town, the whole community was flooded by that same river.

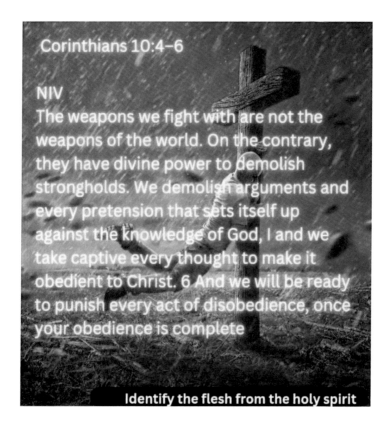

Corinthians 10:4–6

NIV
The weapons we fight with are not the weapons of the world. On the contrary, they have divine power to demolish strongholds. We demolish arguments and every pretension that sets itself up against the knowledge of God, I and we take captive every thought to make it obedient to Christ. 6 And we will be ready to punish every act of disobedience, once your obedience is complete

Identify the flesh from the holy spirit

God
will
never
let you
waste
a step.

AFTERWORD

T he lord of the universe put us together to create this book for humanity by working collaboratively, utilising our different knowledge, skills, signs and wonders. This book will help heal humanity and bring God and Jesus Christ back into the hearts and minds of all men, women, and children if you allow it.

This book is about your personal connection to the creator and Jesus Christ. We do not specifically identify with any religion as such as we share a connection to the creator through our hearts and the actions we take daily.

We have pre-recorded messages below from everyone that worked on "Identify the Flesh from The Holy Spirit" to all the readers of this holy book.

May the peace of God be with you!

Voice messages - please visit the links below.

Gideon E Samson
https://voca.ro/11unX0CIDxul

Olivia Samson
https://record.reverb.chat/s/lQG08Fqr0E99yHcZOLnm

Michael Strachan
https://voca.ro/15Z2CGj0w5B6

Qyntavius Andrews
https://record.reverb.chat/s/Ieocu Ka11YRAxwNCvcl9

Contacts
Emails: avengerfreefromsin@gmail.com

Telegram
freefromsin@telegram
@ApostlSamson-telegram
@forgive4you-telegram
@Angelmichael17-telegram

Table of Contents